Heaven
and Earth
LEADER GUIDE

Heaven and Earth
Advent and the Incarnation

Heaven and Earth
978-1-7910-2903-6
978-1-7910-2904-3 *eBook*

Heaven and Earth: Leader Guide
978-1-7910-2905-0
978-1-7910-2906-7 *eBook*

Heaven and Earth: DVD
978-1-7910-2909-8

Also by Will Willimon

Don't Look Back

Listeners Dare

God Turned Toward Us

Preachers Dare

Fear of the Other

Who Lynched Willie Earle?

The Holy Spirit

Stories

Resident Aliens

Will Willimon

Heaven *and* Earth

ADVENT *and the* INCARNATION

LEADER GUIDE

Abingdon Press | Nashville

Heaven and Earth
Advent and the Incarnation
Leader Guide

Copyright © 2023 Abingdon Press
All rights reserved.

978-1-7910-2905-0

MANUFACTURED IN THE
UNITED STATES OF AMERICA

CONTENTS

CONTENTS

ABOUT THE
LEADER GUIDE WRITER

The Rev. Michael S. Poteet is an ordained Minister of Word and Sacrament in the Presbyterian Church (U.S.A.). A graduate of the College of William and Mary and Princeton Theological Seminary, he serves the larger church as a Christian education writer, biblical storyteller, and guest preacher. You can find his occasional musings on the meetings of faith and fiction at http://www.bibliomike.com.

To the Leader

In *Heaven and Earth: Advent and the Incarnation*, Will Willimon challenges readers to wrestle anew with Scripture traditionally heard during the Advent season. "You've got four weeks to adjust to the jolt of God taking time for us," he writes in his introduction. "So brace yourself. God is on the way."

This Leader Guide is offered as a resource to help you guide a small group in your congregation through Willimon's book, that you all may more fully and deeply observe Advent. As Willimon's book makes clear, keeping Advent is much more than a matter of "being spiritual." It means committing and recommitting ourselves to the God who has decisively committed to us in Jesus Christ, even if that divine commitment sometimes makes us squirm. Willimon insists, time and again, that God loves us too much to leave us alone. His readings of what we might call "familiar" Advent texts encourage us to consider unfamiliar, sometimes uncomfortable, but potentially life-changing understandings of them—insights that can help us grow as Jesus's faithful followers.

In this Leader Guide you will find four sessions, each based on a chapter of *Heaven and Earth*.

Session 1: Meanwhile

Willimon guides readers through Jesus's apocalyptic sermon in Mark 13, daring us to consider how and why God wants to "shake up" the world, the church, and our individual lives.

Session 2: Surprised

Willimon reintroduces readers to John the Baptist as he appears in Mark's Gospel, and calls us to explore how John's message of repentance and conversion matters today.

Session 3: Light

Willimon takes readers from the lofty heights of the prologue to John (1:1-18) to the down-to-earth witness of John to Jesus (1:19-28) and prompts readers to dare imagine themselves as those who can and must testify to Jesus.

Session 4: Rejoice

Willimon strips the sentimentality Christians have let accrue to the story of the Annunciation (Luke 1:26-38) and the Magnificat (1:39-55) so readers might take their place alongside Mary and Elizabeth as Spirit-filled, prophetic singers of God's power and grace.

Adapt and modify the session plans in this guide to craft your small group study. Each session plan includes these elements:

Session Goals—A list of outcomes for the lesson to guide your selection of topics and questions for discussion.

Biblical Foundation—The key Scripture texts Willimon discusses in each chapter of his book, which form the basis of the lesson.

Before Your Session—Practical checklists to ensure you are ready for each group gathering.

Opening Your Session—Icebreaker questions and simple activities to "prime the pump" for your group's discussion.

Watch the Video—If using the accompanying video segments (on DVD or streaming via Amplify Media), watch and briefly discuss each one near the beginning of your sessions.

Book and Bible Study—This section forms the heart of each session. It contains a number of discussion questions about the key Scripture passages and the insights in this chapter of *Heaven and Earth*. You will likely not have time to use them all. Choose the ones you think will connect the most with your group, without being afraid to push them beyond their comfort zones (as Willimon insists God pushes us). Don't ask any questions you are not willing, as leader, to answer yourself, in order to model honest discussion. Have plenty of questions ready to ask, but remain flexible enough to follow your group's discussion where it leads—while also keeping discussions from unhelpful tangents. (No one said leading a church discussion group would be easy!)

Closing Your Session—Questions and instructions are provided for a simple closing discussion or activity focused on a specific passage from *Heaven and Earth*.

Opening Prayers and Closing Prayers—Read these prayers aloud, or pray one of your own.

Optional Extensions—Suggestions for expanding on the session through further research, discussion, or activity beyond the meeting space conclude the chapter.

Thank you for answering the call to lead your group's study of *Heaven and Earth*! May it help make this Advent season an exciting, unsettling, joy-giving, faith-increasing time—and not this Advent season only, but all those to come until the Lord comes.

HELPFUL HINTS

Preparing for Each Session

- Pray for wisdom and discernment from the Holy Spirit, for you and for each member of the group, as you prepare for the study.
- Before each session, familiarize yourself with the content. Read the study book chapter again.
- Choose the session elements you will use during the group session, including the specific discussion questions you plan to cover. Be prepared, however, to adjust the session as group members interact and as questions arise. Prepare carefully, but allow space for the Holy Spirit to move in and through the group members and through you as facilitator.
- Prepare the space where the group will meet so that the space will enhance the learning process. Ideally, group members should be seated around a table or in

a circle so that all can see one another. Movable chairs are best so that the group easily can form pairs or small teams for discussion.

Shaping the Learning Environment

- Create a climate of openness, encouraging group members to participate as they feel comfortable.
- Remember that some people will jump right in with answers and comments, while others need time to process what is being discussed.
- If you notice that some group members seem never to be able to enter the conversation, ask them if they have thoughts to share. Give everyone a chance to talk, but keep the conversation moving. Moderate to prevent a few individuals from doing all the talking.
- Communicate the importance of group discussions and group exercises.
- If no one answers at first during discussions, do not be afraid of silence. Count silently to ten, then say something such as "Would anyone like to go first?" If no one responds, venture an answer yourself and ask for comments.
- Model openness as you share with the group. Group members will follow your example. If you limit your sharing to a surface level, others will follow suit.
- Encourage multiple answers or responses before moving on to the next question.
- Ask: "Why?" or "Why do you believe that?" or "Can you say more about that?" to help continue a discussion and give it greater depth.

- Affirm others' responses with comments such as "Great" or "Thanks" or "Good insight"—especially if it's the first time someone has spoken during the group session.
- Monitor your own contributions. If you are doing most of the talking, back off so that you do not train the group to listen rather than speak up.
- Remember that you do not have to have all the answers. Your job is to keep the discussion going and encourage participation.

Managing the Session

- Honor the schedule. If a session is running longer than expected, get consensus from the group before continuing beyond the agreed-upon ending time.
- Involve group members in various aspects of the group session, such as saying prayers or reading the Scripture.
- Note that the session guides sometimes call for breaking into smaller groups or pairs. This gives everyone a chance to speak and participate fully. Mix up the groups; don't let the same people pair up for every activity.
- As always in discussions that may involve personal sharing, confidentiality is essential. Group members should never pass along stories that have been shared in the group. Remind the group members at each session: confidentiality is crucial to the success of this study.

TIPS FOR ONLINE MEETINGS

Meeting online is a great option for a number of situations. When circumstances preclude meeting in person, online meetings are a welcome opportunity for people to converse while seeing one another's faces. Online meetings can also expand the "neighborhood" of possible group members, because people can log in from just about anywhere in the world. This also gives those who do not have access to transportation or who prefer not to travel at certain times of day the chance to participate.

One popular option is Zoom. This platform is used quite a bit by businesses. If your church has an account, this can be a good medium. Google Meet, Webex, and Microsoft Teams are other good choices. Individuals can obtain free accounts for each of these platforms, but there may be restrictions (for instance, Zoom's free version limits meetings to 40 minutes). Check each platform's website to be sure you are aware of any such restrictions before you sign up.

Video Sharing

For a video-based study, it's important to be able to screen-share your videos so that all participants can view them in your study session. The good news is, whether you have the videos on DVD or streaming files, it is possible to play them in your session.

- All of the videoconferencing platforms mentioned above support screen-sharing videos. Some have specific requirements for assuring that sound will play clearly in addition to the videos. Follow your videoconferencing platform instructions carefully, and test the video sharing in advance to be sure it works.

- If you wish to screen-share a DVD video, you may need to use a different media player. Some media players will not allow you to share your screen when you play copyright-protected DVDs. VLC is a free media player that is safe and easy to use. To try this software, download at videolan.org/VLC.

- *What about copyright?* DVDs like those you use for group study are meant to be used in a group setting in real time. That is, whether you meet in person, online, or in a hybrid setting, Abingdon Press encourages use of your DVD or streaming video.

- *What is allowed:* Streaming an Abingdon DVD over Zoom, Teams, or similar platform during a small group session.

- *What is not allowed:* Posting video of a published DVD study to social media or YouTube for later viewing.

- If you have any questions about permissions and copyright, email permissions@abingdonpress.com.

- The streaming subscription platform Amplify Media makes it easy to share streaming videos for groups. When your church has an Amplify subscription, your group members can sign on and have access to the video sessions.

- Visit AmplifyMedia.com to learn more.

Training and Practice

- Choose a platform and practice using it, so you are comfortable with it. Engage in a couple of practice runs with another person.

- Set up a training meeting.
- In advance, teach participants how to log in. Tell them that you will send them an invitation via email and that it will include a link for them to click at the time of the meeting.
- For those who do not have internet service, let them know they may telephone into the meeting. Provide them the number and let them know that there is usually a unique phone number for each meeting.
- During the training meeting, show them the basic tools available for them to use. They can learn other tools as they feel more confident.

During the Meetings

- **Early invitations.** Send out invitations at least a week in advance. Many meeting platforms enable you to do this through their software.
- **Early log in.** Participants should log in at least ten minutes in advance, to test their audio and their video connections.
- **Talking/not talking.** Instruct participants to keep their microphones muted during the meeting, so extraneous noise from their location does not interrupt the meeting. This includes chewing or yawning sounds, which can be embarrassing! When it is time for discussion, participants can unmute themselves. However, ask them to raise their hand or wave when they are ready to share, so you can call on them. Give folks a few minutes to speak up. They may not be used to conversing in web conferences.

Meanwhile

Session Goals

This session's Scripture readings, discussion, and prayer will help participants:

- articulate their understanding of Advent's significance;
- appreciate the character of Jesus's apocalyptic sermon in Mark 13 and consider its potential to "shake up" their lives and the church today;
- cultivate an expectation of divine intervention in human problems and divine disruption of our plans;
- reflect on patience as a "cardinal Advent virtue" and identify ways to wait patiently but actively for Christ; and
- consider Psalm 46 as an expression of Advent themes.

Biblical Foundation

[Jesus said,] "In those days, after the suffering of that time, the sun will become dark, and the moon won't give

17

its light. The stars will fall from the sky, and the planets and other heavenly bodies will be shaken. Then they will see the Human One coming in the clouds with great power and splendor. Then he will send the angels and gather together his chosen people from the four corners of the earth, from the end of the earth to the end of heaven.

"Learn this parable from the fig tree. After its branch becomes tender and it sprouts new leaves, you know that summer is near. In the same way, when you see these things happening, you know that he's near, at the door. I assure you that this generation won't pass away until all these things happen. Heaven and earth will pass away, but my words will certainly not pass away.

"But nobody knows when that day or hour will come, not the angels in heaven and not the Son. Only the Father knows. Watch out! Stay alert! You don't know when the time is coming. It is as if someone took a trip, left the household behind, and put the servants in charge, giving each one a job to do, and told the doorkeeper to stay alert. Therefore, stay alert! You don't know when the head of the household will come, whether in the evening or at midnight, or when the rooster crows in the early morning or at daybreak. Don't let him show up when you weren't expecting and find you sleeping. What I say to you, I say to all: Stay alert!"

—Mark 13:24-37

God is our refuge and strength,
    a help always near in times of great trouble.
That's why we won't be afraid when the world falls apart,

> *when the mountains crumble into the center of the sea,*
> *when its waters roar and rage,*
> *when the mountains shake because of its surging*
> *waves....*
>
> *Come, see the LORD's deeds,*
> *what devastation he has imposed on the earth—*
> *bringing wars to an end in every corner of the world,*
> *breaking the bow and shattering the spear,*
> *burning chariots with fire.*
> —*Psalm 46:1-3, 8-9*

Before Your Session

- Carefully and prayerfully read this session's Biblical Foundation, more than once. Consult a trusted study Bible or commentary for background information.
- Carefully read the introduction and chapter 1 of *Heaven and Earth.* Take notes about ideas and questions you have as you read.
- You will need Bibles for in-person participants or screen slides prepared with Scripture texts for sharing, or both; newsprint or a markerboard and markers (if meeting in person); video for session 1 (DVD or streaming from Amplify Media); newspapers and magazines.
- If leading a virtual or hybrid session, test your video-conferencing technology.

OPENING YOUR SESSION

Welcome participants to this study of *Heaven and Earth* by Will Willimon. Invite volunteers to speak briefly about why they chose to participate and what they hope to gain from this study. Communicate your own excitement about and hopes for the study.

Ask participants:

- What do you think about and associate with the season of Advent? Why?
- How is Advent like or unlike the season of Christmas? How do you see these similarities and differences in church observances of it? What about in the larger culture?
- How important is observing Advent? Why?
- Reflecting on Advent as "the church's New Year," Willimon writes, "It's not within our own power to make a fresh start." How much do you agree or disagree with this idea, and why?

Opening Prayer

Eternal and eternally creative God, in Jesus Christ's coming you show your determination to make a new beginning with us, and to make new creations of us. As we enter another Advent season in study and prayer, show us where, how, and in whom you are stirring, that we may welcome the newness you give, and live all our seasons faithfully expecting the time you will bring your good will for us and the world to completion. Amen.

WATCH THE VIDEO

Watch this session's video. Invite volunteers to respond:

- What was something you heard that you strongly agreed or disagreed with, and why?

- What was something you wished Willimon had said more about, and why?

Keep the video in mind as well as the book and Biblical Foundation passages throughout your discussion below.

BOOK AND BIBLE STUDY

Apocalyptic Jesus Shakes All Things Up

Recruit a volunteer to read aloud Mark 13:24-37. Ask participants what words or images most captured their attention as they listened, and why.

Have all participants turn in their Bibles to Mark 13. Point out that the Scripture participants just heard is only the end of Jesus's chapter-long apocalyptic teaching—as Willimon notes, "Jesus's longest sermon in Mark's Gospel."

Define *apocalyptic* as prophetic and revelatory speech about the future end of the world. Give participants time to read or skim Mark 13. Once they have done so, discuss:

- What prompts Jesus's apocalyptic sermon (see 13:1-4)?
- What connections can you make between verses 24–37 and Mark 13 as a whole? How do these connections affect the way you hear and understand those verses?
- How comfortable do you feel reading and using apocalyptic images? Why?
- Willimon writes it's "disconcerting to have Jesus say to us...that this world (that we've worked reasonably well to our advantage) is terminal" and that "we are profoundly unsafe" (see vv. 24-25). Do you agree? Why

or why not? What about the world makes you feel "profoundly unsafe"? What, if anything, do or can you do about it?

- Willimon charges that much about the mainline North American Christian experience is "church twisted into a means of keeping our world safe from the cosmic shakings of Jesus." How do you respond? How do you imagine your congregation would react were Jesus to tell visitors admiring your building, "Not even one stone will be left on another"?

- "Apocalyptic Jesus refuses to allow God to be used as the cement of social conformity," writes Willimon, "or to have the gospel trimmed down to common sense." What are some examples, in your judgment, of God and the gospel being used and abused in these ways? What are you doing or could you do in response?

- For "people on the bottom or at the margins" of society, writes Willimon, "Jesus's apocalyptic is good news. Help is on the way." To what extent is this apocalyptic message good news for you and your community? How is your congregation bringing or working to bring embrace and response to this good news?

- Willimon says preachers, rather than worrying about "troublemakers" in the church, "ought to be more worried about all those who are just bored to death." How, if at all, does your church bore you? Bore others? As Willimon asks, "Is there not something within you that yearns to be all shook up?"

God, Intervening and Involved

Ask a volunteer to reread Mark 13:26–27 aloud. Discuss:

- Who is "the Human One" ("Son of Man," NRSVue)? How and why does this One intervene at the end of the world (compare with Daniel 7:13–14)?

- "Maybe there was a day when we could expect divine intervention, but that was a long time ago. We couldn't get the modern world going without first securing ourselves safe from God's agency." What evidence does Willimon point to that the modern world doesn't expect divine intervention? Do you believe God intervenes in the world today? If so, what form does God's intervention take? If not, why not?

- Willimon argues that much modern preaching and churchgoing focus on self-help and self-improvement: "Look at us, we've got the whole world in our hands." How much do you agree or disagree with his assessment? Why?

- "On most days," writes Willimon, "the majority of people in my church can solve most of our problems and meet most of our challenges on our own." How do we determine what problems and challenges, if any, it is appropriate and healthy for Christians to meet on their own? When, if ever, does expecting divine intervention become a problem in itself?

- What is the difference between expecting God to solve all of our personal and social problems, and affirming

God wants to be and is involved in all our problems and challenges?

- "Behind [Jesus's] strange, interventionist, apocalyptic talk," writes Willimon, "is a countercultural claim: If things are set right between us and God, God's got to do it." How do you try to set things right with God on your own? How different would your life look if you took the claim that only God can do so more seriously? What about your congregation's life?

- "Apocalyptic Advent accuses us not of having asked too much of God, but rather of having settled for too little." When and how, specifically, have you "settled for too little" from God? What about your congregation?

- Fred Craddock's story of the preacher surprised by his prayer's efficacy raises the question: when and how, if ever, has God surprised you by answering a prayer in a way you didn't expect?

- "Funny how the Christmases past that I most vividly remember," muses Willimon, "were those when there was some unexpected disruption of our plans." When and how have disrupted plans made your Christmases past memorable? How can these memories help you better appreciate the disruptive message of Advent?

- Willimon tells of another pastor who said, "I wanted to try something so big, so out-of-the-box that if God wasn't in it, if God refused to bless it, we'd fall flat on our faces." What is the biggest, most out-of-the-box something your congregation has tried? What happened? What other big, out-of-the-box things do you dream of your congregation doing to see God's will done? How are you working to make those dreams reality? How do you discern the extent to which God is in these dreams?

Staying Awake and Alert for the End

Ask a volunteer to reread Mark 13:28-37 aloud. Discuss:

- Jesus used the image of a blossoming fig tree to tell his first disciples how they would know the Human One's coming was near. What have you read or heard people mention as signs of the end? What do you think about such suggestions?
- Jesus said "this generation [would] not pass away" before the apocalyptic events he foretold took place (v. 30). How do we make sense of his words two thousand years later?
- Jesus also said not even he knew the end's appointed time (v. 32). How does or should his own freely confessed ignorance on this issue shape our own attitudes toward it? Why?
- Willimon writes that "waiting for God to show up is one of the most challenging aspects of staying in love with God." Do you agree? Why or why not?
- Willimon identifies patience as "a cardinal Advent virtue...the faithful willingness to wait...to let Christ enter our time in Christ's own good time." How is patient waiting for Christ different from patiently waiting for

Christmas? How do you practice cultivating patience for Christ in Advent? How does your congregation do so?

- How does Willimon suggest the delay of the promised end may be good news? What do you think of his suggestions? What others, if any, would you add?

- Willimon notes Jesus repeats the admonition "Keep awake!" three times (vv. 33, 35, 37 NRSVue). How does the parable Jesus tells about the absent homeowner and his slaves illustrate this instruction? What "job" has God given you to do in (as Willimon writes) "the meantime, between Christ's first Advent and the Second"?

- Willimon notes that waiting patiently for Christ doesn't mean we "have to wait with nothing to do." He tells stories about a medical researcher, a church in Trenton, and the Baby Welcome program at an inner-city congregation he served, all of which illustrate faithful waiting for Jesus. Whose stories can you tell that illustrate faithful waiting?

CLOSING YOUR SESSION

Psalm 46 isn't a traditional Advent Scripture, but Willimon quotes several verses from it in this chapter. Read these verses aloud together from the book, or read the entire psalm aloud together from Bibles. Read aloud from *Heaven and Earth*:

> "Times of great trouble" can be, in God's hand,
> seasons of deliverance, though there may be some
> "devastation" and "shattering" in the meanwhile.
> Bad news for those who've trusted in the bow,

spear, and chariot; good news for those who've got
no refuge and strength except God.

(*Optional*) Distribute newspapers and magazines. Invite participants to find images they think could illustrate this psalm. (In a hybrid or virtual setting, encourage participants to look for images on the internet as needed.) Invite volunteers to show their image to the group and explain why they chose it.

Discuss:

- When was a time, if ever, you felt the world, or your world, was falling apart? Where, if anywhere, did you find "refuge and strength"?
- How has God turned "times of great trouble" for you or someone you know into a "season of deliverance"?
- Who are those you would identify as "those who've got no refuge and strength except God"? From what, if anything, would God need to deliver you for you to identify yourself in this way?

Closing Prayer

Come, Lord Jesus. Come and shake us out of our sloth and complacency. Come and shake us out of our apathy toward those this old-and-broken world leaves hurting and helpless. Come and startle us into new and sustained attention at the signs of your presence here and now. And even though we do not grasp the magnitude of that for which we pray, and even though your answer may make us feel as though the very stars are falling, still, we pray: come, Lord Jesus, for only your coming can set us all free. Amen.

Optional Extensions

- Sing or listen to a recording of the African American spiritual "My Lord, What a Morning." How would you describe the spiritual's attitude toward that morning? How does it compare to your own?
- Listen to musical settings of Psalm 46 while participants select images to illustrate the psalm. How do these settings communicate the psalm's messages? Which ones do participants find most meaningful, and why?

SESSION 2

Surprised

Session Goals

This session's Scripture readings, discussion, and prayer will help participants:

- reflect on their experience or lack of experience of physical wilderness;
- identify how and why Mark's account of John the Baptist's ministry (Mark 1:1–8) evokes, and is continuous with, God's previous history with Israel;
- explore what John's message of baptism, repentance, and conversion may mean for today's church, their congregation, and themselves;
- discuss how John the Baptist's announcement in the Book of Mark of "one stronger to come" points to Jesus; and
- practice contemplative reading of Scripture using Psalm 139.

Biblical Foundation

The beginning of the good news about Jesus Christ, God's Son, happened just as it was written about in the prophecy of Isaiah:

Look, I am sending my messenger before you.
He will prepare your way,
a voice shouting in the wilderness:
"Prepare the way for the Lord;
make his paths straight."

John the Baptist was in the wilderness calling for people to be baptized to show that they were changing their hearts and lives and wanted God to forgive their sins. Everyone in Judea and all the people of Jerusalem went out to the Jordan River and were being baptized by John as they confessed their sins. John wore clothes made of camel's hair, with a leather belt around his waist. He ate locusts and wild honey. He announced, "One stronger than I am is coming after me. I'm not even worthy to bend over and loosen the strap of his sandals. I baptize you with water, but he will baptize you with the Holy Spirit."

—Mark 1:1-8

LORD, you have examined me.
You know me.
You know when I sit down and when I stand up.
Even from far away, you comprehend my plans.
You study my traveling and resting.
You are thoroughly familiar with all my ways.
There isn't a word on my tongue, LORD,

that you don't already know completely.
You surround me—front and back.
    You put your hand on me.
That kind of knowledge is too much for me;
    it's so high above me that I can't reach it.

Where could I go to get away from your spirit?
    Where could I go to escape your presence?
If I went up to heaven, you would be there.
    If I went down to the grave, you would be there too!
If I could fly on the wings of dawn,
    stopping to rest only on the far side of the ocean—
        even there your hand would guide me;
        even there your strong hand would hold me tight!
If I said, "The darkness will definitely hide me;
    the light will become night around me,"
    even then the darkness isn't too dark for you!
        Nighttime would shine bright as day,
        because darkness is the same as light to you!

You are the one who created my innermost parts;
    you knit me together while I was still in my mother's
    womb.
I give thanks to you that I was marvelously set apart.
    Your works are wonderful—I know that very well.
My bones weren't hidden from you
    when I was being put together in a secret place,
    when I was being woven together in the deep parts
    of the earth.
Your eyes saw my embryo,
    and on your scroll every day was written that was
    being formed for me,
        before any one of them had yet happened.

> *God, your plans are incomprehensible to me!*
>> *Their total number is countless!*
> *If I tried to count them—they outnumber grains of sand!*
>> *If I came to the very end—I'd still be with you.*
>> *—Psalm 139:1-18*

Before Your Session

- Carefully and prayerfully read this session's Biblical Foundation, more than once. Consult a trusted study Bible or commentary for background information.

- Carefully read chapter 2 of *Heaven and Earth*. Take notes about ideas and questions you have as you read.

- You will need either Bibles for in-person participants or screen slides prepared with Scripture texts for sharing; newsprint or a markerboard and markers (if meeting in person); video for session 2 (DVD or streaming from Amplify Media).

- If leading a virtual or hybrid session, test your video-conferencing technology.

OPENING YOUR SESSION

Welcome participants. Ask any group members who've had a "wilderness adventure"—however they define it, from a pleasant overnight camping trip to "roughing it" for weeks at a time (or longer)—to talk briefly about their experiences. Discuss:

- Why do some people seek wilderness adventures? Why do some people avoid them?

- What creature comforts would you (or did you) miss most during a wilderness adventure?
- With what real or fictional stories of wilderness adventure are you familiar, from books, TV, or movies? Do you enjoy these stories? Why or why not?
- What life lessons can wilderness adventures teach that may be difficult, if not impossible, to learn in other ways?

Read aloud from *Heaven and Earth*: "Advent is announced not in some beautifully proportioned church, but in the remote, untamed, uncivilized wilderness where it's hard to find your way, and some become lost....Advent is a wilderness adventure."

Opening Prayer

God Most High, God Most Free: How quickly and casually we try to tame your Word! How desperately we imagine your message must conform to our comfort, rather than hear how urgently you call us to conform to the cross of your Son. By your Spirit, may this study help us prepare your way in our hearts and lives this Advent, that we may find ourselves, at this season's end, ready not so much for Christmas as for a new and even wild experience of Christ. Amen.

WATCH THE VIDEO

Watch this session's video. Invite volunteers to respond:

- What was something you heard that you strongly agreed or disagreed with, and why?
- What was something you wished Willimon had said more about, and why?

Keep the video in mind as well as the book and Biblical Foundation passages throughout your discussion.

BOOK AND BIBLE STUDY

"In the Beginning" All Over Again

Recruit a volunteer to read aloud Mark 1:1-8, while other participants listen. Invite participants to share their impressions of John the Baptist. Encourage them to note whether what they think about John is present in Mark's text, or whether it may come from some other source. Discuss:

- "In opening his Gospel with 'the beginning,'" writes Willimon, "Mark says the advent of Christ is Genesis 1 all over again." Why does Mark begin his account as "Genesis 1 redone"?

- Willimon distinguishes "news" from other types of messages (for example, "secret knowledge" or "rules and regulations"). How do you know or judge when something is news? How do you determine true news from false, and "good news" (v. 1) from bad?

- "John [the Baptist] is a bridge from the Old Testament to the New." Compare verses 2-3 with Isaiah 40:3 and Malachi 3:1. What claims does Mark make about John by linking him to these Old Testament texts? What claims does Mark make about God?

- What Old Testament stories do you remember (or can you find in your Bible) about how God's people experienced the wilderness? (Examples include

Exodus 16; Numbers 14:1-25; 1 Kings 19:1-8). How do these scriptural echoes affect the way you hear and understand Mark's account of John's ministry?

- "For Israel after the Exodus," writes Willimon, "the wilderness was a place of testing—tests that Israel often flunked." How might John's ministry represent another test for God's people? When was a time your congregation faced such testing—and how did it do? How have you faced such testing in your own life?

- Why does Mark describe John's appearance (v. 6; compare 2 Kings 1:8; Zechariah 13:4)? How is John like and unlike other prophets in Scripture?

- "The Incarnation…is not God's novel act of desperation when everything else God tried before didn't work.…Jesus's advent is not God's Plan B after God's Plan A failed." How does the way Christians understand the relationship between the Old and New Testaments affect how we read the Bible? how we think about and seek to serve God?

Preparing for a Lifetime of Surprise and Change

Recruit a volunteer to read aloud again Mark 1:4-5. Discuss:

- What are the most demanding preparations you've made? Did your preparing serve you well—or do you yet know? When was a time you wished you'd made more preparations than you actually did? What happened?

- "When someone responds to the church's Advent announcement with 'God has never shown up to me,' it's not unreasonable to say, 'Maybe God has, but you weren't prepared to be surprised.'" When and how has God surprised you? your congregation? How is it possible to prepare for surprises from God?

- What did preparing the Lord's way look like for John and those who went to the wilderness to hear him? What does it look like today for you? for your congregation?

- Willimon writes, "Baptism means everything that water means...in the name of Christ. God's word in water" (see pp. 50–51 for a discussion of these meanings). Which of baptism's many meanings that Willimon identifies is most meaningful for you, and why? Which one, if any, most surprises you, and why? How much or how little does your congregation's baptismal practices communicate these meanings?

- In baptism, says Willimon, God uses "ordinary, bodily stuff of mundane creaturely life"—water—"to get through to us." Baptismal water isn't inherently special, but by grace becomes sacramental. When else have you experienced God's love through the ordinary stuff of creaturely existence? How might we prepare ourselves to be more open to such sacramental encounters with God?

- "In baptism, you are not the sole author of the narrative of your life." Regardless of how old you were when you were baptized (if you have been), how have you changed and grown into the identity you received? How do you think you still need to grow into it?

- "John preaches baptism before he speaks of repentance because repentance...is not something that you do but rather something God does in you." Do you agree? Why or why not? What is our responsibility in repentance?

- Willimon offers AA as an example of dramatic changes that accompany God's gift of repentance. What are some examples you can offer, from your own or others' experience?

- "There's no way to begin worshipping Jesus without ceasing our bowing and scraping to some false god." What idols have you had to abandon (or might you still need to abandon) to worship Jesus? How does or how could your congregation help you?

- "Nowadays," Willimon observes, "we seem to have lost faith in the ability of the Holy Spirit to change hearts and minds." If you agree, how can we restore such a faith? If you don't agree, where have you seen and do you see evidence to the contrary?

- Willimon describes John's message as one of "regime change." "Come on," writes Willimon, "make King Herod nervous. Be baptized, begin being the revolution." Have you ever made anyone nervous—authorities, family members, friends, fellow Christians—because you have heeded the call to repentance and conversion? Does your congregation make anyone nervous as you all follow Christ? If so, who? If not, why not—and how could it start?

- "Though the rite of baptism takes only a few minutes to perform, it takes your whole life to finish what was begun in you." How seriously does your congregation take its responsibility to help the baptized grow into their identity their whole lives long? What more could it be doing?

One Who Is Greater Is on the Way

Recruit a volunteer to read aloud again Mark 1:7-8. Discuss:

- What does John say about the one for whom he is, as Willimon puts it, "the advance man, the announcer, the one who warms up the audience before the star attraction"?

- Compare John's announcement in verses 7-8 with those in Matthew 3:11-12 and Luke 3:16-17. Willimon notes, "Mark's Baptizer preaches grace rather than judgment." What do we gain from reading multiple accounts of John's message in the Gospels? How would you describe the relationship between grace and judgment?

- Read Matthew 11:2-6. "Even John," writes Willimon, "...is surprised that the One who came was powerful in a different way from the Messiah he expected." Have you ever shared John's surprise about Jesus? What do you do with such questions?

- "Jesus didn't just preach the gospel; he was the gospel." What does the Incarnation tell us about who God is and how God acts? What does it tell us about who God expects the church, the body of Christ, to be?

- Willimon advises, "Prepare for the advent of Christ by locating yourself as close as you can to where Christ is likely to show up." Where are those places? How can we know? How often and consistently do you and your congregation locate yourselves there? How are you or can you locate yourselves there this Advent season?

CLOSING YOUR SESSION

Read aloud from *Heaven and Earth*: "There's never been a better poem to describe what God's up to than Psalm 139. I'm sure that John the Baptist, and most of those to whom John preached, knew this psalm by heart. From the cradle to the grave, we can't be rid of God's seeking, searching love."

Lead participants in a brief, focused reading of Psalm 139:1-18. Invite participants to close their eyes and listen for a single word or phrase that captures their attention. Read the verses slowly but steadily. Ask participants to name the word or phrase that stood out to them.

Instruct participants to listen for what God may be calling them to do or to be in response to the psalm. Read the verses a second time and, after two or three minutes of silence, ask how they feel God wants them to respond.

Closing Prayer

Loving God, where indeed can we go from your presence, when you were pleased for your presence to dwell among us, as one of us, in Jesus Christ? Help us prepare, we pray, for fresh and surprising experiences of your grace, that we may welcome your gift of repentance. Transform us and work within us so that, when we come to our very ends, we will still be with you. Amen.

Optional Extensions

- Willimon mentions the first-century CE (AD) author Flavius Josephus, calling him "the turncoat Jewish historian." In between sessions, interested participants may want to research Josephus, his significance for biblical studies, and why Willimon would call him a "turncoat" and report back briefly to the group during Session 3.

- Invite pastoral staff to talk about how and why your congregation's baptismal practices developed as they have. Discuss whether any changes might allow for fuller expression of baptism's meanings when the rite is performed.

SESSION 3

Light

Session Goals

This session's Scripture readings, discussion, and prayer will help participants:

- remember and reflect on the role preaching has played in their Christian faith;
- appreciate the unique ways in which the Fourth Gospel emphasizes John who baptizes as a "witness to the Light";
- consider the nature and purpose of Christian preaching;
- explore what it means to be a witness to and give testimony about Jesus; and
- express written thanks to someone who has been a witness to Christ for them, and consider those for whom they might be witnesses to Christ this Christmas.

Biblical Foundation

> *In the beginning was the Word*
> *and the Word was with God*

> and the Word was God.
> The Word was with God in the beginning.
> Everything came into being through the Word,
>   and without the Word
>   nothing came into being.
> What came into being
>   through the Word was life,
>   and the life was the light for all people.
> The light shines in the darkness,
>   and the darkness doesn't extinguish the light.

A man named John was sent from God. He came as a witness to testify concerning the light, so that through him everyone would believe in the light. He himself wasn't the light, but his mission was to testify concerning the light.

—John 1:1-8

This is John's testimony when the Jewish leaders in Jerusalem sent priests and Levites to ask him, "Who are you?"

John confessed (he didn't deny but confessed), "I'm not the Christ."

They asked him, "Then who are you? Are you Elijah?"

John said, "I'm not."

"Are you the prophet?"

John answered, "No."

They asked, "Who are you? We need to give an answer to those who sent us. What do you say about yourself?"

John replied,

> "I am a voice crying out in the wilderness,
>> Make the Lord's path straight,
>> *just as the prophet Isaiah said."*

Those sent by the Pharisees asked, "Why do you baptize if you aren't the Christ, nor Elijah, nor the prophet?"

John answered, "I baptize with water. Someone greater stands among you, whom you don't recognize. He comes after me, but I'm not worthy to untie his sandal straps." This encounter took place across the Jordan in Bethany where John was baptizing.

—John 1:19-28

Before Your Session

- Carefully and prayerfully read this session's Biblical Foundation, more than once. Consult a trusted study Bible or commentary for background information.
- Carefully read chapter 3 of *Heaven and Earth*. Take notes about ideas and questions you have as you read.
- You will need either Bibles for in-person participants, or screen slides prepared with Scripture texts for sharing, or both; newsprint or a markerboard and markers (if meeting in person); video for session 3 (DVD or streaming from Amplify Media); paper and pens or pencils.
- If leading a virtual or hybrid session, test your audiovisual and videoconferencing technology.

OPENING YOUR SESSION

Welcome participants. Ask them:

- What memories, if any, do you have of past Christmas sermons you've heard?
- Is there one sermon, out of all the sermons you've heard as a Christian, that stands out most in your memory? Why has that sermon stuck with you?
- How important have preachers and their sermons been in shaping your faith? Why?
- How would you define or describe the purpose of Christian preaching?

(If you happen to be one who preaches to your participants, you may need to actively encourage honesty and practice humility!)

Read aloud from *Heaven and Earth*: "During the season of Advent, the Fourth Gospel says that a major way you gain access to an encounter with [God's Word made flesh] is through the human voice of a preacher out in the wilderness, 'a man named John.'"

Tell participants this session considers John the Baptist as a preacher, and every Christian today—preachers or not—as those who can and do also bear witness to Christ.

Opening Prayer

God of wonder, too often we fail to hear the good news of your coming in Christ as news. Use this time of reading and reflection to surprise us again. Help us hear the voice of your servant John, crying out about your true Light coming into the world. Open the eyes of our heart to see glimmers of your incarnate Word's glory, here and now. Teach us how to speak about and respond to Jesus's advent as news—good news—once again. Amen.

WATCH THE VIDEO

Watch this session's video. Invite volunteers to respond:

- What was something you heard that you strongly agreed or disagreed with, and why?
- What was something you wished Willimon had said more about, and why?

Keep the video in mind as well as the book and Biblical Foundation passages throughout your discussion below.

BOOK AND BIBLE STUDY

From Heaven to Earth

Recruit a volunteer to read aloud John 1:1-8 (or, as time allows, 1:1-18), while other participants listen. Discuss:

- John (the evangelist) uses two rich metaphors in his Gospel's prologue: Word and Light. How does he use each image? What associations do these images have for you? What other images, if any, can you think of to convey what John wants to convey about Jesus in these verses?
- Willimon says each of the New Testament Gospels talks about Christ's coming (advent) "in order to make a claim

about the God/human Jesus, but also to be honest about us and the limits of our imaginations." What claims does John make about Jesus in his prologue? How does John challenge your imagination's limits?

- "The bold Christian claim is that when we look at this Jew from Nazareth…we see as much of God as we ever hope to see.…[Jesus] is the whole truth about God." What difference does (or ought) this claim make to the way we think about God? To what we say and do in God's name? To how we respond to competing claims about God?

- Willimon notes John's prologue quickly shifts from "the ethereal and heavenly" to "the solid stuff of God's good earth." How does (or ought) this downward movement shape Christian spiritual practices?

- Do you think Willimon was right to dismiss the idea of the students' proposed Spirituality Center in Duke Gardens? Why or why not? How does your congregation emphasize "the solid stuff of God's good earth"?

- Do you agree that "heaven's movement, thanks to the Holy Spirit, is always downward, one-way traffic from God to humanity"? Why or why not?

- "The Word, which is not self-evident, is prone to incomprehension and misunderstanding," writes Willimon (1:10-11), yet "at least in the Fourth Gospel, Jesus seems unperturbed and undeterred by people's lack of comprehension of his words." Why did God choose the risky method of an enfleshed Word to communicate with the world (1:14)? What does (or ought) God's incarnate conversation with the world in Jesus mean for our conversations with the world as Christians today?

- "We weren't opposed to Jesus until he opened his mouth. His words brought out the worst in us. Jesus told us the truth about God and we hated Jesus for it." When and how does the truth Jesus told about God still bring out the worst in people—including and especially Christians?

A Voice Sent from God to Preach

Recruit volunteers to read aloud John 1:19-28, taking the roles of the narrator, John, and his questioners, while other participants listen. Discuss:

- Why does it matter that John "was sent from God" (1:6)?
- What possible identities for John do verses 19-21 consider and reject? How would you answer the question in verse 22 about yourself, were someone to press you for a clear, declarative word about who you are?
- In the other three Gospels, the evangelists identify John as the "voice crying out in the wilderness" (v. 23) from Isaiah. In the Fourth Gospel, John identifies himself as that voice. How, if at all, does this difference shape your understanding of John's identity and purpose in the Fourth Gospel?
- Willimon argues preachers today "are successors to John.... A preacher is sent, speaks under external authorization and compulsion, and delivers a word that does

not originate with the preacher." How near or far is Willimon's understanding of a preacher to your own understanding? Do you agree preachers are not "finally accountable" to their congregations? Why or why not?

- Willimon asserts the Incarnation "is the great mystery that makes preaching possible." What does he mean? How is preaching "an incarnational, God/human, Spirit/flesh exercise"?

- An African American preacher told Willimon, "Preaching is about getting people to a place where Jesus can get to them and they can get to Jesus." When was a time, if ever, that preaching accomplished this goal for you?

- In the Fourth Gospel, Willimon notes, John's preaching is "inviting people to see the Light, assuming that if he could just get listeners to look in the right direction, they would know how to respond to what they see." What implications does John's preaching have for Christian preaching today?

- "Hearing, really hearing a sermon requires external assistance. God, Father, Son, and Holy Spirit saying words to us through a preacher that we could never say to ourselves." When, if ever, have you told a preacher you "really heard" their sermon, and what did you tell them you heard? How did the preacher respond?

- How, specifically, does your congregation encourage your preacher(s) to preach in ways that "enable the risen Christ to walk among his people" (Bonhoeffer)?

Called to Be Witnesses

Recruit a volunteer to read aloud John 1:29-34, while other participants listen. Discuss:

- What qualities make someone a good witness? Have you ever served as a witness or had to testify in a legal proceeding? What was the experience like? What happened as a result of your testimony?

- Willimon writes that we are called to witness not only "to the advent of the Babe of Bethlehem" but also "to be witness to what we've seen and heard…to testify to the reality of an event that has occurred, a gift that has been given." How is being a witness to and giving testimony about Jesus like and unlike serving as a witness in a legal setting?

- "The Messiah is not a concoction of our wishful thinking," writes Willimon. "The gospel is not something that we come up with by ourselves." How do we determine whether the witness we bear and the testimony we give is faithful and true? Have you ever wondered or worried whether the gospel is wishful thinking? How do you deal with such questions if and when you have them?

- Willimon writes, "Love is rarely love if it's fully comprehensible. Loving and being loved by Jesus is a lot like that." Has the truth that love for and by Jesus isn't fully "comprehensible" ever kept you from bearing witness to it? If so, how? If not, how do you deal with its "incomprehensibility" and deliver testimony nonetheless?

- When and how do you or have you served as a witness to Jesus? How comfortably do you think of yourself as Jesus's witness? Why?
- What forms of witnessing to Jesus does your congregation emphasize most? least? Why?
- "John the Baptizer doesn't sit in Jerusalem, keep office hours, and welcome people to God. John goes out to the wilderness to them." How are your and your congregation's witness to Jesus informed by John's example?

CLOSING YOUR SESSION

Read aloud from *Heaven and Earth*:

> How did you get here in church, exploring the mystery of the Incarnation? You are here only because someone "sent from God" told you the truth about Christ....There was a person sent from God whose name was Amy (or Tom, or Barry, or June, or _____). The witness was nobody special....But for some reason, the Light chose not to shine without the testimony of the witness.

Ask participants to think about whose name they would choose to fill in the blank in Willimon's sentence, and why. Distribute paper and pens or pencils to those who need them. (In virtual or hybrid settings, encourage remote participants to get paper and a pen or pencil.) Invite participants to write a brief note or letter of thanks to the witness they are thinking of—whether the witness is living or dead, whether the participant wants to or could send or deliver the letter. Encourage participants to tell the witness how, specifically, the witness pointed them to Jesus, and what concrete difference that testimony has made. Invite volunteers who wish to read or summarize their letters for the whole group to do so.

Read aloud from *Heaven and Earth*:

> Think about someone you know…who needs some good news, someone who has not yet gotten the message that God is with us. How about inviting that person to join your church as it celebrates Christmas Eve? Christmas Eve is usually church at our best. Why don't you be a witness to the good news by inviting someone to join us as we stand in wonder before the grand mystery of the Incarnation?

Invite participants who are willing to talk about (not necessarily identify by name) who they will invite to your congregation's Christmas services. (Note: If you choose to include this activity, you must be ready to talk about the person you will invite to Christmas worship!)

Closing Prayer

O Lord, you have given us the gift of language, that with it, we may give you praise. And beyond mouths that can share words, you have given us hands that can share food and caring touches, and feet that can carry us to all the wilderness places where someone waits to experience your loving presence through us. By your grace, send us to testify, in word and deed, to the Light who shines on all people, whose glory we have seen in Jesus Christ, your Word made flesh. Amen.

Optional Extension

- Invite a preacher from another congregation and denomination or tradition to take part in your discussion. (Offer to rearrange your schedule for this session if needed.) Ask them to react to the views of preachers and preaching Willimon expresses, and to talk about their own understanding of their role.

Rejoice

Session Goals

This session's Scripture readings, discussion, and prayer will help participants:

- consider how Luke's story of the Annunciation depicts God's determination to be "uncomfortably close" to humanity, as well as God's power to bring possibilities out of impossible situations;
- reflect on how they, like Elizabeth and Mary, have been or are now being called to speak or act prophetically;
- listen to the Magnificat as Mary's "clench-fisted battle cry" and identify ways God might be calling them to shake up their lives and world through it; and
- rejoice together in song to celebrate the good news of Advent and Christmas.

Biblical Foundation

When Elizabeth was six months pregnant, God sent the angel Gabriel to Nazareth, a city in Galilee, to a virgin who was engaged to a man named Joseph, a descendant of David's house. The virgin's name was Mary. When the angel came to her, he said, "Rejoice, favored one! The Lord is with you!" She was confused by these words and wondered what kind of greeting this might be. The angel said, "Don't be afraid, Mary. God is honoring you. Look! You will conceive and give birth to a son, and you will name him Jesus. He will be great and he will be called the Son of the Most High. The Lord God will give him the throne of David his father. He will rule over Jacob's house forever, and there will be no end to his kingdom."

Then Mary said to the angel, "How will this happen since I haven't had sexual relations with a man?"

The angel replied, "The Holy Spirit will come over you and the power of the Most High will overshadow you. Therefore, the one who is to be born will be holy. He will be called God's Son. Look, even in her old age, your relative Elizabeth has conceived a son. This woman who was labeled 'unable to conceive' is now six months pregnant. Nothing is impossible for God."

Then Mary said, "I am the Lord's servant. Let it be with me just as you have said." Then the angel left her.

Mary got up and hurried to a city in the Judean highlands. She entered Zechariah's home and greeted Elizabeth. When Elizabeth heard Mary's greeting, the child leaped in her womb, and Elizabeth was filled with the Holy Spirit. With a loud voice she blurted out, "God has blessed you above all women, and he has blessed the child you carry. Why do I have this honor, that the *mother of my Lord should come to me? As soon as I heard your greeting, the baby in my womb jumped for joy. Happy is she who believed that the Lord would fulfill the promises he made to her."*

Mary said,

> *"With all my heart I glorify the Lord!*
>> *In the depths of who I am I rejoice in God*
>> *my savior.*
>> *He has looked with favor on the low status of his servant.*
>>> *Look! From now on, everyone will consider me*
>>> *highly favored*
>>>> *because the mighty one has done great things*
>>>> *for me.*
>> *Holy is his name.*
>>> *He shows mercy to everyone,*
>>>> *from one generation to the next,*
>>>> *who honors him as God.*
>> *He has shown strength with his arm.*
>>> *He has scattered those with arrogant thoughts*
>>> *and proud inclinations.*
>> *He has pulled the powerful down from their thrones*
>>> *and lifted up the lowly.*
>> *He has filled the hungry with good things*
>>> *and sent the rich away empty-handed.*
>> *He has come to the aid of his servant Israel,*
>>> *remembering his mercy,*
>>> *just as he promised to our ancestors,*
>>>> *to Abraham and to Abraham's descendants*
>>>> *forever."*

—*Luke 1:26-55*

Before Your Session

- Carefully and prayerfully read this session's Biblical Foundation, more than once. Consult a trusted study Bible or commentary for background information.
- Carefully read chapter 4 of *Heaven and Earth*. Take notes about ideas and questions you have as you read.
- You will need either Bibles for in-person participants or screen slides prepared with Scripture texts for sharing, or both; newsprint or a markerboard and markers (if meeting in person); video for session 4 (DVD or streaming from Amplify Media); paper and pens or pencils.
- Either handouts or screen slides of Luke 1:46b-55, or both, to ensure all participants can read from the same Bible translation.
- If leading a virtual or hybrid session, test your audiovisual and videoconferencing technology.

OPENING YOUR SESSION

Welcome participants. Ask:

- What is your favorite Christmas carol or hymn, and why? (List carols and hymns named on newsprint or markerboard.)
- What is an especially powerful memory you have that is associated with Christmas music?
- Last session, you were asked to remember meaningful Christmas sermons. Is remembering meaningful Christmas music easier or harder? Why?

List responses on newsprint or markerboard.

Read aloud from *Heaven and Earth*:

> I'm all for preaching like that of John the Baptizer, but sometimes our faith is better sung than said....Luke's prelude to Christmas occurs in an obstetrics waiting room that's been transformed into a musical theater.

Tell participants this session will explore one of Luke's "Christmas carols" and the context in which it is sung.

Opening Prayer

O God, who spoke all things into being, and who spoke your Word made flesh in Jesus: You have always called your people to sing for joy. As we approach the end of our Advent study, may we join the endless, heavenly chorus that praises your name. By your Spirit, may we rejoice so deeply in your salvation that all our words and deeds magnify you. Amen.

WATCH THE VIDEO

Watch this session's video. Invite volunteers to respond:

- What was something you heard that you strongly agreed or disagreed with, and why?
- What was something you wished Willimon had said more about, and why?

Keep the video in mind as well as the book and Biblical Foundation passages throughout your discussion.

BOOK AND BIBLE STUDY

Announcing an Uncomfortably Close Advent

Recruit three volunteers to read aloud Luke 1:26–38, taking the roles of the narrator, Gabriel, and Mary, while other participants listen. Discuss:

- The story of Gabriel's visit to Mary is so familiar in Christian tradition it has its own name, "the Annunciation." What, if anything, in the story still manages to capture your attention and imagination—or what about it, if anything, makes it uncomfortable?

- What is significant about the way Elizabeth's pregnancy frames this story (vv. 26, 36)? What, if anything, do we lose when we sing about or see art depicting the Annunciation outside of this "frame"?

- What do you think and feel about Mary's first response to Gabriel (v. 34)? What about her second (v. 38)? Can you identify with one of these responses more than the other? Why or why not?

- How is Mary's initial "doubt, pondering, and wonderment," even "disbelief," different from Zechariah's when he learned of Elizabeth's pregnancy (Luke 1:18)—or is it? Why is Zechariah silenced, while Mary will shortly sing about the good news?

- Do you think either Elizabeth or Mary could have said or considered saying no to God's plans for their miraculous pregnancies? Why or why not?

- Gabriel tells Mary, "Nothing is impossible for God" (v. 37). Do you take the angel at his word? Why or why not?

- Willimon mentions some situations—drug addiction, churches' shrinking budgets and membership—that "seem intractable" and hopeless, "unless Gabriel's words are true." What are some impossible situations—in your world, your community, your congregation, your own life—where you need or want to hear Gabriel's promise?

- How does the story of the Annunciation depict God, in Willimon's words, "show[ing] up, com[ing] close, get[ting] all mixed up in our humanity"? What difference does God being "down and dirty with us" and "uncomfortably close" make in your life? in your congregation's life?

- "If God could show up to these two otherwise unknown women, God could show up to anybody, anywhere. Even to you, even to me, even here, even now." When and where, if ever, has God shown up to you? How do you know? How did you respond?

- Why does Willimon say Jeremiah 24:7—"They will be my people, and I will be their God"—is either a promise, a command, or an invitation, or more than one of these, depending on one's perspective? How do you hear this divine declaration? Why?

- In what ways were Elizabeth and Mary pushed to the margins in their society? Who gets pushed to the margins today? Why does Willimon say these people should "pay careful attention to this Advent story"?

- "God's determination to be God for the whole world is accomplished by calling a few particular people to be witnesses for God." How does Willimon find this movement in both the Old and New Testaments? What might

God's habit of calling a few for the good of all mean for your congregation? Your denomination?

Called to Be Unknown Prophets in Unknown Places

Recruit a volunteer to read aloud Luke 1:39-45. Discuss:

- What do we discover about the Holy Spirit when Elizabeth "blurt[s] out" her prophetic speech (vv. 42-45)?
- When, if ever, have you relied, voluntarily or otherwise, on God's Spirit to give you words to speak? What happened when you spoke?
- "Nobody has to be faithful to the Holy Spirit's vocation on their own." How can we recognize or know when the Spirit is with us, equipping us to answer God's call to be Christ's disciple?
- Willimon tells the story of an affluent attorney washing dishes at an inner-city congregation of people who are homeless, who told him he did so because "Jesus insisted." Whom have you known who has done something for the same reason, "whether [they] liked it or not"? Have you ever done something because Jesus insisted? What was it? Would you do it again?
- When, if ever, have you suggested how God might be leading someone to take specific action? How did the person respond to your suggestion? What happened?
- Willimon encourages us to hear these two otherwise unknown women's story as maybe our own, because "most of us are unknown to the world." Do you hear Mary and Elizabeth's story as yours? How so? If not, why not?

- "Judea is nobody's idea of the center of the universe," writes Willimon. "And Nazareth is the outback of Judea." What does God's decision to honor an unwed, pregnant woman (and likely a teenager) as the mother of God's Son, the Messiah and Lord, in such a place suggest about God? What might it suggest about such places today?

- Willimon suggests that "during Advent, we all live in Nazareth." What does he mean? Do you agree? Why or why not?

- "God surprised Mary and Elizabeth by showing up where they were and making things happen to them in order to make good things occur in the world. Be careful to whom you open your door." When, if ever, have you or your congregation unexpectedly opened your door to God Almighty, showing up in your unknown corner of the world, intent on making something happen? Did you help make God's plan happen, get in the way, or stand on the sidelines? How and why?

Mary's "Clench-Fisted Battle Cry"

Have all participants read together (in unison, or alternating verses) Luke 1:46b–55. Discuss:

- Like "the Annunciation," Mary's words are known by their own name, the Magnificat (the first word in Latin translation). How would you describe this text's tone? What words, phrases, or images most captured your attention? What did they make you think or feel?

- Pretend for a moment the Magnificat were the only part of Scripture you had. What would you know about God from it alone? What would you think and feel about this

61

God? Would you want to worship and serve this God? Why or why not?

- "The song that Mary sings is no sweet lullaby," writes Willimon; "it's a clench-fisted battle cry." How does Mary describe "the revolution that Jesus brings to the world"? How do you react to Mary's news that "God has taken sides"?

- "By singing her song in the past tense," notes Willimon, "...Mary implies that God was not performing some surprising new work that is out of character for God." What Old Testament stories can you think of that confirm the Magnificat's image of God?

- "Christ came into our world as it is," Willimon writes of Jesus, "but refused to leave it as it was." How did Jesus fulfill the promises in Mary's song? How does Jesus continue to fulfill these promises?

- "Mary's song is good news for some, bad news for others." How do you hear it, and why? What, if anything, might you do to hear it differently?

- "God has chosen" not to "shake up God's world... without the assistance of ordinary folk like Mary, Elizabeth...and maybe even you." Where might God be calling you to shake up your life and perhaps even the world? How will you discern and confirm this call?

CLOSING YOUR SESSION

Thank participants for having shared this study of *Heaven and Earth* with you. Invite volunteers to talk briefly about something they gained from the study, or about some question they will take with them. Be prepared to do so yourself.

Read aloud from *Heaven and Earth*:

> Lay aside this book and pick up a hymnbook. Get
> on to the serious business of Christmastide—your
> joyful singing. There will be other sermons and
> Sundays when you are given a tough assignment by
> Jesus like loving your enemies or praying for those
> who persecute you. Here, at the end of Advent
> and the beginning of Christmas, it's different. You
> are given a gracious invitation: Rejoice!"

Closing Prayer

As your closing prayer, sing one or more of your group's favorite Christmas carols or hymns together, identified when you began this session.

Optional Extensions

- Listen to one or more musical setting of Mary's Magnificat. Look in your hymnal for hymns based on it, and sing one or more of them together. How well does each musical setting you listen to or sing capture the meaning of Mary's words, as you understand them after this session?
- As Willimon notes, Mary's song "is not original." Compare and contrast Mary's song with Hannah's song in 1 Samuel 2:1-10. (Review 1 Samuel 1 for its context.) How does reading these two songs together increase your insight into each, and into God's revolutionary ways?
- Take your group Christmas caroling, especially in a setting where the group can also serve those hearing the carols in some tangible way.